STRANGE
ENCOUNTER

A. L. ROWSE

STRANGE ENCOUNTER

JONATHAN CAPE

THIRTY BEDFORD SQUARE LONDON

FIRST PUBLISHED 1972
© 1972 BY A. L. ROWSE

JONATHAN CAPE LTD, 30 BEDFORD SQUARE, LONDON WCI

ISBN 0 224 00699 1

PRINTED IN GREAT BRITAIN
BY RICHARD CLAY (THE CHAUCER PRESS) LTD
BUNGAY SUFFOLK

To Colin Wilson for his faith

Poetry is a piece of very private history, which unostentatiously lets us into the secret of a man's life.

Thoreau

Contents

Preface

I have been asked to say something about the relation of my poetry to the history that I usually write, but I find this extremely difficult. Perhaps it will be easier for me to approach it from the outside, and say that the combination of poet and historian is strangely rare — strange, for there is no contradiction between the two activities. Many poets have been dramatists or novelists, essayists or critics. But I can think of only two who have combined poetry with history: Samuel Daniel, in the Elizabethan age, was a poet who wrote good history; Macaulay, in the Victorian, was a historian who wrote better verse than is sometimes appreciated.

Some friendly critics regard me as a poet who happens to write history. Indeed, I began to write poetry much earlier and have continued to do so all my life — this is my sixth volume, in my sixth decade. When I began, as a schoolboy in Cornwall, very much on my own with no one to guide or help, I fancied myself as a Celt and an offshoot of the Irish school I admired, Yeats, Synge, Padraic Colum — one of my first poems was called 'Ireland' — as in later years I admire the poetry of W. R. Rodgers and Louis MacNeice.

The dominant influence for my generation, however, was Eliot, who published my work, was a constant encouragement, inspiration, and friend. He once told me that he could only write verse if he regarded it as a problem to be solved (he was a great one for crossword puzzles). It was quite the opposite with me: I only write verse when emotionally moved or, at any rate, in a certain mood. He was once kind enough to say that it came closer in feeling to his own than any of his professed followers, but I had a deep sympathy for the man as well as for his poetry, though earlier (and perhaps more constant) influences were Hardy and Swift.

I sometimes make the distinction that history represents my public, poetry my private, self — and it was long before I could bring myself to publish my poetry at all. Perhaps the distinction is a superficial, if convenient, one; for history, with the greatest historians, has often been illuminated by the glow of poetry, while poetry has often been inspired by the sense of the past, the poignant intuition of the transcience of life that comes to one in sudden moments of revelation.

Perhaps this is where the two join — I cannot see any conflict between them or why the conjunction should be so incomprehensibly rare. They are two aspects of one experience, two modes of apprehending the mystery of life: the one more intellectual and descriptive, the other more intuitive and probing, more searching and disturbing. Perhaps that is why I could not give myself wholly to the writing of poetry as Eliot wished: too disturbing, though it came more naturally. Writing history, though an effort of the will, was easier on the emotions, made for a more bearable life — searing enough in our time, with all we have gone through, in any case.

There is an advantage in being a historian, to set against the disadvantage of having one's poetry disregarded by those who haven't noticed the rarity of the conjunction. Nothing dates so quickly as the 'contemporary'. An eminent American poet, a friend of mine, recently had a good poem of his rejected by our leading literary journal on the ground that it had no contemporary message. Shakespeare was not much interested in the contemporary (though very much in the past, the most historically-minded of dramatists) — but he was no worse a poet for that; Ben Jonson was very much concerned with the contemporary — but he was no better a poet for it. The plain fact is that such a criterion is irrelevant to art: the only test is whether the poem is authentic and good.

The historian is more than usually aware how soon the 'contemporary' is dated. Much of the work of the thirties, by my contemporaries, who made this the chief intention of their verse, is already dead. The poet of them all whose work is most likely to survive is Louis MacNeice, who was least concerned to be 'contemporary'. A classical scholar, he knew what lasts. To be contemporary is to be a journalist – the very words are analogous – and much modern verse is really journalism.

Perhaps it is here again that the historian and the poet come together, in perceiving that the test of art is closely related to that of time, that time winnows out the authentic in literature from what is merely contemporary. And a historian should know how to wait.

Trenarren,   A.L.R.
Summer 1971.

Trinity Sunday

STONEYARD, boneyard, haunt of the loved shadows,
Bells ring out over the deserted meadows,
And it is Trinity Sunday — Becket's favoured feast,
Martyr and madman — parish feast of my childhood:
Upright stands the scaffolding, upright the dome,
Home of dead friends, and my last home.

Flag ripples from flagpole in the June breeze,
Wagtail searches the lawn: no trees
In this gaunt wilderness of stone,
Corniced, Corinthian-columned and swagged
With flowers and wreaths of stone all flagged:
Birdsong in the silence when the bells have ceased,
First Sunday in June, unforgotten Trinity feast.

Portrait of a Scholar

WHEN I hear the sighing sound of Magdalen
 Chime, I think of Bruce and the mystery
Of time, some thought of the fifteenth century
He inhabited all his working life;
Of Boarstall Grange surrounded by its moat
We looked down upon from Elsfield and Stow Wood
Where we walked, and I listened to the flood
Of information about Bastard Feudalism,
The facts behind medieval chivalry,
The predatory finances of Sir John Fastolf,
The truth about Courtly Love, clean contrary
To C. S. Lewis's legend and *parti pris*.
Or paying a call on Chaucer's granddaughter, Alice,
Duchess of Suffolk, in her chapel in Ewelme church,
Above the meadows where the cresses grow,
The chalk-stream of ragwort and rare mimulus.
Or again we are walking up the Cherwell Valley
To Tackley church, to see a familiar friend
Dead five hundred years: I watch Bruce bend
Over the cold marble monument
To print a kiss upon the icy brow —
I forget of whom that sleeps in the tomb,
Some member of the Lancastrian house with collar of esses
Whom Bruce knew like any contemporary.
And now they share alike time's mystery.

Dover Pier

WHO is this shadow beside me in the walks
Always present though he never talks,
At least I never hear him but with inner ear,
Never see, yet he is nearer than if here,
More near and dear for passing beyond the known
Into the unknown where I cannot follow till I die?
He shadows me down Addison's Walk to Dover Pier
Whose name he told me once when we were here.
The strangeness of it! — to sense his presence
Yet cannot conjure him in the flesh to my side,
Ask him questions, see his smile, hear his replies.
Yet he suggests to my open mind he knows
My grief, accepts it as sincere,
Waits for me on the other side of the weir.
The water passes under the bridge as when he was here
And crushed the leaves of autumn underfoot —
No footfall now — we exchanged the news of summer,
Confronted the prospects of winter,
Commented with malice on the passers-by
Vanishing down the leaf-strewn avenues
As when he — here or not here now — was here.

Mayday Surprise

'EGOCENTRIC, eccentric, he will name a cat
   Peter' – thus Auden: myself
Stares out at me from the printed page.
And yet once more I have missed May morning,
Not even heard the bells of Magdalen,
Merely the merry voices of morris-dancers
Returning in Queen's Lane.
O Mayday, come yet once again
For me that I may once in a lifetime
Arise with the dawn, go down the High
To the Bridge, the waters of time moving by
While we await the signal from on high.
But by what unconscious telepathy
Should Wystan have sent this Mayday
Message, traced the fact about my cat and me,
Faced me with myself this May morning
In unexpected printed charactery?

A Forgotten Soldier

Gay and casual and discontinuous,
  Taking life and women as they come —
Who is that waiting at the gate for the nurse-girl
When you told me you were going on leave?
Faithless and feather-headed as a bird,
Tethered by no sense of obligation,
Changeable like the weather or the sea:
Here is the source of your unconscious charm,
Young pouf from the London streets,
To whom your old bachelor friend would give
Money, without ever making a demand on you —
You could not understand it, so you said.
Sex or love or gratitude: nothing of these
Meant anything to you, earning your bread
From hand to mouth, from one to another day by day:
Hanging round the Park for a pick-up,
Scrounging a pittance for a meal,
In return for your unregarded body
You set little value on. Then the Army
Caught up with you, taking away
Any care or thought for what may come.
Where are you now?
I doubt if you survived those years ago,
Fighting in the Desert, in Sicily, or at Anzio,
Fulfilling in your fate your last words to me:
'That is a thing I could never understand,
Why anybody should break their heart about me.'

Grantham

THE soaring spire of Grantham
Is graven in my heart
From ways we went together
Before we drew apart.

All of eastern England
Spreads out on either side:
The tender green of pastures,
The meadows grave and wide.

Here a drift of primroses,
There a fruit-tree white:
All in the April evening,
The soft and shadowed light.

At top of the rise a church,
A flag flies from the tower;
The village crouches round about,
Awaiting the Easter hour.

On the slope the sheep are feeding,
A pheasant crops among,
In the dip the pale green willows
Trail misty veils along.

In a cutting silver birches
Catch a gleam of sun
That falls on folds and gables
Just before day is done.

All this we loved together,
But now the years have flown:
Absence and separation
Upon us both have grown.

The country we used to visit
Vanishes from the train
With love, with life, the ways
We shall not walk again.

Strange Encounter

IN the sharp November air of Armistice day
I make my way through the churchyard, not to pray
But remember the generations that trod this path
Through the centuries before — to push open the door
And find myself alone in the silence of the church.
Thus early in the morning, no one there.
Moved, and yet unmoved to prayer,
I turn and find I am alone with a corpse.
The silence is listening, comes alive: who is there?
Who is it there under the folded pall,
Heavy with silence, as if aware
Of the stranger here, afraid of his own footfall
For fear it awake the dead. The stillness has ears:
The silence finds tongue in the candles flickering
At head and foot, as all through the night.
And now it is morning, no one to care
But the stranger, strangely moved in the half-light,
All unbelieving, goes through the motion of prayer
For one all alone: 'As you are now, whoever you are,
So shall I be, nor the time long ere I am as you.'
So saying, I draw away from the bay,
Afraid to remain close to whoever is there,
Perambulate the church still and grey in the chill
Morning air, moving further away from the bier,
In the shadows the flickering tongues of flame
Still following me, to where the Rood looks down
In pity and charity on him alike and me.

But why none of his family to watch and pray,
Why no one to wake the body its last day
On earth but the stranger, perhaps led this way
All unexpected and unknown to him or me?

Beneath the Rood I learn the dead man was a priest
Brought here for his last night to be spent
Beside the font where he ministered:
Perhaps it is meant I am to wake him,
Was sent to receive his benediction unknowing.
In the silence I thought I heard him sigh,
'And all is well, and all shall be very well.' And I
Ceased to fear to be in the company of the dead,
Of the priest awaiting his requiem, such as may be said,
I hope, though unbelieving, nevertheless for me.
All around me the sweetness and the silence
Dedicated to the dead, softly I withdraw,
Leaving him there alone with the Rood
To the absolution of solitude.

Looking up to the Chilterns

THE downs today are silver-green and thistle-grey,
   The water meadows punctuated by coloured cattle,
The heave of hill marked by prehistoric barrow
Tufted by a tree, the islanded waste
A mass of purple loose-strife and pink willow-herb.
O dark green waters and hills draped with trees,
Arms extended in blessing upon the land,
The scarlet poppies lighting up the corn,
Grey towers in clustered villages
Nestling in the crevices of the hills,
Chalk streams running down from the Chilterns,
Summer at its height in cedars and fringed willows,
Towering chestnuts and delicate spired poplars:
O all ye green things upon the earth,
                        bless ye the Lord;
O all ye works of the Lord,
                        bless ye the Lord.

Near Boconnoc

IN spite of being given to words
I never have been able to express
Fully the sense of life at heart,
Find the right words for the mystery.
But then, who can?
All poets' words are but a charactery,
Notes traced on the margins of experience.
I stand at a gateway in silence
At the ecstasy of swallows over a field of wheat,
White-bellied, black-glittering, darting and diving,
Wheeling and skimming, a tumult of wings,
With the wind rippling in waves
Across a landscape all silver and green:
And underneath the mounded barrows and the graves.

Trewarne

Lapped in the leaf-filtered sun
  Lies the grey house of Trewarne,
Looking down the valley to the mill
That clacks no more busily to the morn.

All is silent in the summer sun,
Fragile leaves on printed walls;
Within the flowered and waiting forecourt,
No foot that falls.

Tread softly: do not arouse the ghosts,
Nor wake the house from its long sleep.
Once, in the time of the Civil Wars,
It was wide awake, and down the slope
The sons of the house, confronting the day,
Buckled their armour and rode away.

A shadow clouds the upper windows
Where child-bed and death-bed alike had place:
In the haunted noontide, when all stands still —
The illusory withdrawal of a face.

What face looks out upon the selfsame scene,
Unchanged between Civil War and now?
The house is empty: behind mullion and lintel
No footfall, no murmur, how
Can there be eyes to watch
For the lifting of the latch?

Enter not: peer in through the panes
At bare hall and beckoning corridor:
Only the motes and dancing sunbeams
Scurry along the floor.

The house is withdrawn within its world
Of memory, nor cares who pass
And, looking within, see only themselves,
Transitory phantoms in mirrored glass.

Ardevora Veor

A T turn of tide, clear sky,
  Seventh September morn,
A boy goes sculling by
Down river from Ruan Lanihorne.

The secret flats of the Fal
Reveal unnumbered birds
Mirrored in quiet waters:
A world still beyond words.

Behind a screen of elms
A deserted house is there,
Haunted by its echo —
Ardevora, Ardevora veor.

A herring-bone hedge of stone,
A lodge at the entrance gate,
An orchard of unpicked apples:
For whom, or what, does it wait?

Evidences of former love
And care on every side,
The anchorage, the quay:
No one comes now at the turning of the tide.

A planted berberis sheds
Its berries on the ground;
From the windlass and the well
No movement ever, and no sound.

The pretty panes are broken,
Blackberries ripen on the wall:
Peer in through the windows,
Whence no one looks out at all.

No one looks out any longer
Across the creek to the farm;
From candle-lit doorway to attic
No signal of joy or alarm.

Nor any motion of footfall
Beneath ceiling or rafter by day;
All laughter, all merriment over,
The ghosts have their way.

A house alone with its shadows,
The floors strewn with sharp glass,
What may have happened here
At Ardevora, Ardevora veor,
What estrangement come to pass?

Only an echo replies
Into the listening morn
As the solitary sculler
Moves silently down river
With the tide from Ruan Lanihorne.

Trenarren Winter

SMOKE rises from cottage chimneys,
The crooked valley comes alive;
Wet roofs among Cornish elms
Shelter the winter hive.

On the way to the headland
The road the cattle pass,
Water in the cart-track
Gleams a ribbon of glass.

And I recall old Ben the bull
Swinging down the lane,
Returning with the herd:
They will not come this way again.

Nor George, the farmer's son,
Who went to sea at Hallane,
While Rover watched the beach
Night and day for a sign:

Who, as a boy, would range the fields,
Dog at heel, gun in hand,
Unconscious of grace and beauty,
Young master of the land.

And master of the girls,
Who have forgotten sooner than I,
Who see him still against the bay
Under a summer sky:

Like the bright day of sun and gale
Scarred in the memory,
The treacherous turn of tide
That swept him out to sea.

New Year in Cornwall

BILLOWING grey-blue sky,
The umbrella pines of Rome,
The grieving seagull cry,
To remind me I am home.

Along the line of ledra,
The winter smudge of browse:
Turn back up the valley
To the lighted house.

A late rook calls a curfew
Over the winter scene;
In the bank a hollow
Where honey-bees have been.

Now over the magic valley
Through the trees' leafless screen
Rises the silver moon,
Ravished but serene;

While over the shoulder of hill
Strikes on the listening ear,
From the navel of the parish,
The last peal of the year.

Summer Siesta

WAKING in mid-afternoon of hot summer,
  Sun and sea patterns printed on the blind,
I hear myself saying, still half in sleep,
'I used to love Rover.' Dear dog dead
I used to hear the valley over, welcoming
The young master, shepherding the cattle home
Up the lane from the headland in the afternoon.
It struck me strangely to remember Rover
Suddenly, years after, dear visitor
Unannounced, his place long taken
By a young successor.
Why was I so disturbed to remember him?
Defenceless, vulnerable in half-sleeping state,
The will suspended that keeps fears away,
Controls the secret anguish of the mind –
Was it his watching the beach night and day
For the vanished master of the ivory skin and ferny hair?
No. It was the unexpected reminder
Of the relentless onward roll of life
Like the unalterable tide across the bay,
The irreversibility of time.
We were younger then when we came here:
The valley was full of youth: the master was alive,
His brother with the sloe-black eyes a boy
About with the cattle in boots too big for him,
Now away on questionable courses,
Never comes home. The farmer and his wife
Are a couple growing old, nothing to do
Who were so active all day long,
Sowing, harrowing, haymaking, harvesting.
No longer the cows come here to be milked,
No Rover to accompany them, in at the gate

With the milk in the fresh of the morning.
One has the sense of everything slowing down.
Youth has gone from the valley;
Only Rover has his sullen successor,
No work to do. I, growing older,
Keep a more solitary vigil
Out over valley, farm and bay,
Remembering their former occupants —
As they perhaps remembered theirs —
Suddenly aroused from summer siesta,
Pierced to the heart with the sense
Of the mysterious continuity of life.

The Beeches at Trenarren

'Let us walk up the road and see the beeches.'
The harmless phrase disturbs the suspended mind —
The road, the lane echoing with the feet
Of so many dead, of my own dead youth,
The eagerness, the ecstasy, the fire,
Sharpness of sensation, on edge with desire.
At Trevissick turn where the road forks
The old folks began to make a carriage-drive:
There the beeches grow, flattened by sea-wind
Like the umbrella pines of the Pincio.
Here, looking out over blue bay, headlands
Brown or green, after-harvest stubble-gold —
The harvesters are all gone into the earth:
Castle Gotha stands witness to the generations
Time out of mind, the ruined rampart,
The home of the silent vanished races
Discoloured earth, a little ash.
How to express the inexpressible
Sense of life, drifting cloud and air,
Of presences in the lane no longer there —
Myself among them — good old Davy,
Stout of heart and strong of arm, nobody
Could manage a roof-ladder like him;
George and Rover dead, Ray gone away,
Debonair and gay, driving his tractor
In the morning uphill to the upper fields,
Or down the lane tired at end of day.
No longer. All has passed into the cave of time,
Silted up like the sands in the bay,
Treasured and numbered, running through the hands
Of the sentinel on these cliffs, keeping his watch,
Overcome with the mystery

Of leaf and lane and tree,
The blue between beeches,
Of sun on sea,
And time and memory.

Distant Surf

'Go round to the front door, and you'll hear
The church bells ringing,' she says.
I obey the call, go up the worn and secret steps
Hollowed out by the generations
To listen up at the back among the beeches.
No longer sharp of hearing, as when a boy
I heard them resonant and loud in the alleys
Of the town, or borne on the west wind
Up to the village, on to the china-clay uplands.
Cupping ear in hand, at last I hear
A faint and distant surf of music on the breeze,
The changes no longer distinct and clear.
But I am pleased amid the melancholy
Wreck of my life — golden glow on the headland,
The rare north light of late summer
Reflected in the north-west, over the upper field
And on the underbranches of the beech-trees,
Upon the big black gate that gives upon
An illusory paradise, so desirable once,
A lonely land, no reverberation of love.
I have lost the distant surf, once so confident,
I have lost my way, navigating towards the end
Without compass or star, without faith or any hope.
Coming indoors, 'Summer is at an end,' I say,
'It is already autumn, it might be September.'
Yet, closing the door upon the world, I am consoled
To think that the church-bells I remember
From childhood can still be heard over the parish,
Out to the uttermost confines,
The headland catching the last light of the sun,
To mingle their distant surf
    with the surf of the darkening sea.

A Dream in Lincoln, Nebraska

SLEEPING uneasily in Lincoln, Nebraska,
Five thousand miles away, I find myself once more
At the clanging gate we used as choirboys
Into the churchyard, fifty and more years ago.
(O the anguish to be sixty and not sixteen again,
O the irreversibility of time!)
There by the vestry door stood the old vicar,
Recognizable as rarely in dream: in faded black,
Flat pancake hat, scrawny neck and Adam's apple,
More a scarecrow than ever, dear dotty Dr Lea.
I was apprehensive, afraid he might not know me,
He must be so very old now, I thought,
At least a hundred I calculated dreaming,
For he was a man of sixty when I was a boy.
He appeared more skeleton than man,
With a couple of wardens, like warders, to hold him up;
Something indecipherable between us in the path,
A mound, perhaps a coffin. As I approached –
The familiar scene from all those years ago,
The path, the vestry door, the darkling church,
The grinning gargoyles looking down, the vicar
Himself one – I said: 'Do you remember me?
I was a choirboy here. I used to sing.'

Fourth Sunday in Lent in Central Park

THE idiot people swing in the sun: baboons
  In the human zoo. Young men spit as they pass,
The dogs lift up their legs and gaily piss.
The primeval rocks are draped with monkey children;
The paths echo with all the tongues under the sun.
Leaves scrattle, squirrels scuttle, bohunks
Rifle the garbage bins; perambulators are propelled,
An old man hugs his unquiet heart.
The bare shadows of the natural world are better
Than all this scum. Balls are caught and thrown,
Returned or purposefully pursued. Dust is blown
Into the eyes and mouth, into the mind and heart.
Dead branches lie, a crimson kite in blue sky
Flutters over the scuffling field.
The bust of Giuseppe Mazzini looks calmly on:
Why is he here? — except to make clear
This is the melting-pot of Europe. A revolutionary
In portentous cape swings bogusly by.
Bicycles circulate. A second-rate orator
Perorates from his pedestal; a Negro speaks
Better sense to his young hopeful: 'Jes you keep
Yer mouth cloased an' you woan't git in noa trouble.'

Here lake water laps, but no church bells chime over the
    water,
No peal rings out to evensong. A sick woman clings
To a bench in the sun, eyes closed, blue veins stand out.
The people hold radios, their bibles, in their hands;
The unbelieving churches rear spires on the edge
Of the Park, where the cliffs of the secular world

Predominate. Here among the rocks the old lags
And poufs congregate. You couldn't come here in the dark.
Shall we descend into the Zoo? No need so to do.
A woman, dressed in dogskin, fondles her dog:
Hard to tell which is woman and which dog;
A yellow-trousered man carries his cat.
Bolívar and San Martín prance on their horses,
Liberating in vain to the unheeding populace:
The coloured crowd is happier on the rink.
Curious to think of skyscrapers, a planetary fringe,
Rolled round in space. The ducks have no idea.

The Music of Humanity

'THE still sad music of humanity':
    Terrible voices tear the air coming up
From pornographic Seventh Avenue,
Awake me in the early hours in the glare
Of neon lights through the squalid slats —
A woman's voice shrieking dementedly,
As it might be Janis Joplin or Bessie Smith,
In altercation with her man, obsessive, hysterical:
The man's voice pleading, then growing angry
With her unreason, going home from some lewd dive.
Drink, drugs, money, sex,
The universal burden of it all.
The screaming voice carries on with their footfall
Echoing down the street, to what terminus?
One night on the pavement of Fifty-Fifth I saw
A well-dressed man administer a blow
Resoundingly across the face of his woman.
She took it unflinching, made no moan.
What was that about? Some female lie,
Some malice from a poison-tongue?
What kind of life is theirs? Drink, drugs, money, sex,
The music of humanity. That voice, that blow,
Echo in my ear and fill the night with fear.

The Strange American

THE sight of heterosexual happiness
Distastes: see them straphanging in the bus,
Two fools seized by a sudden impulse to smother
Each other with kisses, leaning over the other,
Exhibitionists in the public eye
With less decorum than animals in a zoo.
They as suddenly desist at the look
Of the observer writing in his book
With the mesmerized fixation of a snake.
The enthusiastic lover looks loftily down,
Asks the stranger to open the window pane
So that his love may breathe a little air.
The man refuses, sits stonily there;
At a second request, 'Try another,' he says.
Taken aback that the man should refuse
A demand made as if conferring a favour,
'A strange American,' he murmurs, the colour
Rising as he returns to his adoring girl.
Finding a seat at last, she adjusts a curl,
Lays a hand superfluously on his knee,
Baring her cage of teeth at him, while he
Bristles his masculine moustache at her.
The moving hand writes on without a stir
Or sign that it has circumscribed the scene.
All is resumed as if nothing there had been.
There appear, from the corner of an envious eye,
Two heads transfigured against the western sky.

Portrait of a German Woman

MONUMENTAL, *unsterblich*, bloody German *Frau*,
Out of whom came the robots who ruined the world,
Hard, unsmiling face, with eyes unseeing,
Turned in upon yourself, rapt
In contemplation of what deadly dream,
What ecstasy of blood and iron, breeding
Sons for *Deutschland, Deutschland über Alles*.
Inconsiderate of ill, under your enormous hat,
Like the Kaiserin's in the Tiergarten
Now shattered in a thousand pieces:
Behind you I see Krupp, Thyssen and Stinnes,
The malign *Macht* that wrecked our century.
Woman with a stance like a Buddha, but evil,
Abstracted from the beauty of the world,
The crimson flowers beside you unheeding:
Yet conscious perhaps of the fate laid on you,
Priestess carrying your unspeakable burden,
Woman of iron, with hands upon your womb,
Woman of the sorrowful face, and of the wrath to come.

Before Cortés

UNDERNEATH man's innate cruelty
  There is his apprehension of beauty
No less strong, inspiring every art
In every form, wood, jewel, stone.
See here the spirit's succession in time,
From Olmec to Maya and Toltec to Aztec.
Observe the mania for ritual, the feeling for proportion,
The holy madness, feeding the blood of humans
To the fire lest the sun should fail to go round.
Here learn the closeness of man to animal:
Man carries a jaguar-cub, struggles with snake,
Celebrates the cult of jaguar and serpent,
For both come out of the caves, the underworld.
Here is the headdress of coyote or plumed serpent,
The priest in flayed human skin for the rites,
The bones of blood-brother ritually burned,
The borne bowl of pulque foaming to the brim,
Sprinkling incense in one hand, knife in the other,
Terebinth and turpentine, resin and cinnamon.
The jewels are ceremonially crushed and thrown
Into the cenote of sacrifice to Quetzalcóatl,
Lord of the Morning, or Xolotl, Evening Star.
The hierophants, in ecstasy, the drugged *danzantes*,
Make their demented moan to two-toned drum,
Tear their flesh with sting-ray spines and thorns,
Blood flowing from human hearts impaled
Upon sharp obsidian knives, the captives
Mutilated before slain in obscene ceremony,
The frightened eyes of the victims, accepting
Their fate, for they too believe.
From the severed neck of the victim, blood flows
In five streams rendered in jade, chalcedony.

C

A terrible beauty is born and reborn
From mad beliefs, made permanent in stone,
All in due order according to the calendar.
These glyphs recount man's madness, record
The appalling distances we have come,
Yet still unslaked beneath the outer skin,
Render the essential cruelty
Under the common humanity.

Middleton Place, Charleston

GONE is the rhetoric of Sumner or Calhoun
That led but to Fort Sumter or Fredericksburg
And ended all at Appomattox —
Gone with the wind that ruffles trees in the park
Named for Francis Marion, patriot of the Revolution,
Who is now no more than a name either.
Who now remembers Moultrie, or Beauregard
Of the dashing looks and cavalry charges,
Or Henry and Arthur Middleton, of Congress
And the Declaration of Independence?
They are better remembered for their garden,
The pleached alleys they planted, the Chinese
Azaleas acclimatized, gingko, mimosa,
Varnish- and spice-trees brought home to Charleston,
The magnolia walk along grass-green water,
The turf terraces that edge shapely ponds,
Native oak, crêpe-myrtle, cherry-laurel,
The spired and pyramidal camellias.
There was the house framed in its formal landscape
Designed by the master and his English gardener.
All was entire before Sherman passed this way,
Left his mark in the burned and ruined flanker,
Spoiling the symmetry that still looks out
Over the acres of lawns and empty rice plantations,
That once sustained the house and the family
Now gathered within the sombre granite vault,
Watched by the darkies sweeping up the leaves,
While spring birds sing their funeral lament.
Still the winged house confronts open river
Running down to the city with its wharves
And harbour, gateway to the ocean sea.

Old Baldy

HERE in the foreground, funereal cypress and palm,
There in the background, the eternal snows:
Old Baldy rears his crest
Above the emerald lights of Arcadia,
Glittering and sparkling in the winter air.
The San Gabriel mountains extend their flanks
Lavender and grape-purple, fold upon fold,
Upheaved from the plain centuries before
The Fathers came to name them for the Faith.
Mount San Antonio to them, white and withdrawn,
Takes on a richer hue from the lost sun
Gone down in the wastes of the Pacific,
Is now no more than a wraith withheld
In its own silences, where the winking plane
Makes an insolent comment upon our uncertain day,
Carefully picks its way around the mountain-mass,
Could easily shatter its frail cargo,
Could crack a nut against the mountain side.
Now only a hooded presence, keeping its vigil —
Suspending its unspoken sentence
On the cities of the plain and their ephemeral life —
Into the oncoming night of no return.

The Forest Ranger

SIM JARVI, the tall forest ranger,
Slim and sun-crowned Finn, died here.
By birth an Oregonian, all his life
He gave to the service of forest and mountain:
Here at Sierra Alta remember him.
He knew the secret lair of mountain lion
And where lurked the black bear: killer
And prey were alike to him, both in his care.
The lion roaring after his prey doth seek
His meat from God. To him each had his place
In the harmony of nature, less red
In tooth and claw than the great killer: man.
His clear blue eye would scan the mountain face,
Detect outlined against blue rim of sky
The big-horned sheep or shy mule-deer.
Racoons would come to him to be fed. Even
The rattler crossing his path had no hurt of him.
He knew all the trails like the veins on his hand,
All the secrets of that upheaved land lay
Open to him: the lateral fronds of white fir,
The silver bark of canyon oak, even
The sharp thorns of buckbrush were his friends.
He loved the rough striations of the rocks,
Black and white like a giant panda, grey
Or burnt umber and ochre, sepia and rose.
Taking a few wafers and raisins, a flask
Of water to quench his thirst, he would quest all day
Under the sun, in and out the cool shade
Of sugar pines, or the stiff Jeffery firs,
The petrified skeletons of trees
Laid waste by lightning or by forest fire.
On such a July day, the noonday sun

Bringing out the resinous scents,
The aromatic odours of manzanita
And yucca — our Lord's candle — he lay down to die,
Alone in the loved high altitudes:
No one around, only a cicada singing,
In the silent solitudes no breath nor sound.
At night a little wind arose to play
With the fronds of his hair and cool his brow there
Where he lay — of your charity remember him —
Under the glittering Californian stars.

The Road to Claremont

FOLLOW along Foothill out into the waste lands
Keeping the mountains in view in the intervals
Of gasoline stations, trailer camps, dead orange groves –
Relics of an earlier culture – with split walnut trees,
Lopped palms looped with electric lights.
Homes! Homes! Homes! Churchill Highlands. College
   Heights.
Camper and Trailer Real Estate on Citrus Avenue.
Et one Brute? – Lay's Potato Crisps.
Gulf. Gulf. Texaco. 76 Minute Man Service.
Dramatic! Distinctive! Daring! – New Chevrolet.
Dallas? – Get Delta's Downy Bird. For Sale
This valuable frontage. *Beautify Our Highways!*
The mountains look down on the desolation,
Torn eucalyptus and stripped palm with disdain.
A frail hibiscus puts forth a flower with no moral.
Subdivision. DEVELOPMENT. P R O G R E S S.
The fallen leaves scrattle on the pavement,
A mountain breeze blows the toyon berries about,
Arbutus fruits batter their blood on the kerb.
Why pay retail for a car loan? *Attend the church of your choice.*
Come winter, come Miami. Happy motoring to all!
Gulf. Gulf. Texaco. 76 Minute Man Service.
No Scotch improves the flavor of water like Teacher's.
Get the best of both in better balanced homes.
City of Glendora, Pride of the Foothills. Don't fence me
   out!
We Rent Tools, Trucks, Trailers. *Beautify*
Our Highways! Throwawayable New Plastic Bottle.
Throw it away into the dying orange grove,
Or by the roadside where the scarlet poinsettias
Light up the smog. At the Christmas corner lot

A monster purple dog arrests attention,
Demeaning the amphitheatre of mountains
Relegated to a backcloth for civilization.
Kitchen Sink on the Blink? Call a P.I.P.E.
Plumber. Robustelli Cars: No Credit Needed:
Bankruptcy O.K. Loosen your seat-belt:
Travel American Lines to New York. Auto Tops,
Cut-rate gasoline. Certified Mortgages. Used Cars.
Hibiscus punctuates the devastation;
Roses and oleander, manzanita and sagebrush
Struggle and expire amid Mobile Homes, Add-a-Room,
The House that Jack Built, Income Unit,
Homes on your Lot, Homes — if that's the word for it —
Choice Mobile Homes. Mount Baldy, Drive-in Theatre,
    Dancing Nitely.
Attend the church of your choice. A citrus grove offers
To be subdivided for shopping centre. Adorable Pets —
Animals Beauty Parlor. Grooming. Poodles clipping.
Don't forget your Zee Napkins. *Beautify Our Highways!*
Concerning this 486 commercial acres contact
Etiwanda Realty. Shady Acres. Trailer Lodge.
Paradise Hills: Exclusive Sites. Homes! Homes! Homes!
Subdivision. DEVELOPMENT. P R O G R E S S.
Housing Lots. Shopping Lots. Mortuary Lots.
Be fruitful and multiply, copulate and die.
Serenity is Nearby at Rosehills Cemetery.

Christmas in California

THERE is the mass of mountains under the moon,
There are the lights of Arcadia, green and gold;
Here the palms and olives, Monterey pines:
How different a landscape as I grow old
From the simple and innocent slopes I knew as a child,
Up the furze-parks to the downs of Carclaze,
Past the claypits and clear pools by the road,
The scent of heather and thyme where the sheep graze:
Carn Grey on the skyline looming over the bay,
The same moon suffusing the coast with its glow
For a boy homeward-bound those years ago,
The moorland scent in nostrils as he mounted the hill
In the sharp air towards Christmas, thinking he still
Saw the star above Bethlehem, the faithful shepherds
Keeping their flocks on a similar night,
The Magi make their pilgrimage all in a row,
As if all the mystery of the Orient were there
Over the rim of the headland bathed in light,
The bay filled to the brim with gold, and not far
The Wise Men, Gaspar, Melchior, Balthasar.

Waiting for the Storm

FRIGHTENED but fatalistic I follow the rain,
    The threatened cloudburst over the mountains,
The ominous sunset into which we go,
Horror in the heart, dying a hundred deaths,
In plane or car swerving on freeway,
Always wondering what end the clouds portend –
The palms await their death-sentence,
The cacti extend their crucified arms –
Apprehensive of any unexpected approach,
Every symbol of reproach on my course,
Caught in blizzard, alarmed at each moment
Of heading off the obliterated road,
The danger that stalks one down the hills:
Life, as a friend found, a track through jungle,
On either hand the panthers waiting to pounce.
The landscape still, now preternaturally dark,
Birds of paradise hold up inquiring heads
Scenting the storm, or rather, the wrath to come,
Though, for the moment, the coast is clear.
How long, O Lord, how long?
We die before we learn to live, just
When we are learning to live it is all over.

Experiment

THIS is the way it will be when I am dead
Lying outstretched full length upon a bed
No superfluous symbol of faith at my head
Yet arms folded across my breast as if
Making a cross unrecognized in life
Duly arranged by a servant: no wife
To grieve or rejoice or anyone else of my kin
Alone with myself at the last as I have lived
Little but contempt for kith and human kind
Alone upon a bed in a strange land
Far from former home and earlier friends
Sped on before me to a common bourne
Leaving the world poorer than it was
Easier to leave than I had ever thought:
Bare arms folded upon the white sheet
No chalice beside me to indicate the priest
No crozier or pastoral staff to show
The shepherd I might have been, symbols of
Childhood dream – dream or dedication
I know not which – now it is all one
As if my vagrant life had never been:
Here lies one whose inner face unseen
Was turned away from light and faith and hope
By some secret wound or ever he was born;
Cover his face, close his eyes for him –
Unregenerate, unafraid –
Upon a world he never made.

Foetus

I COIL up in bed, a foetus in the womb,
Or primitive burial in a tomb.
The bitter light of Fifty-Fifth Street
Filters through slats on the white sheet
Into the sick room lit with flowers,
Where I lie and count the hours
Until I am home again by the sea,
And all that is then left of me
May be consigned to mother-earth:
A likelier, shapelier rebirth
Than this crouched figure in the womb
Seeking a premature, alien tomb.

December 4th, 1969

THE train ploughs slowly through the frosted fields,
And I am sixty-six today. 'The infirmities
Of sixty-six are coming on me,' wrote Samuel Drew,
My cobbler-townsman, antiquary and theologian.
No theologian I: a disillusioned humanist.
The cooling towers of a generating station
Dwarf the Thames Valley I knew as a boy
Coming first to Oxford. Looped wires and stalking pylons
March now across meadow and pasture,
Up chalk hills to Chilterns and the Downs
Of old Tom Hughes and the Scouring of the White Horse
Above lanterned medieval Uffington.
The filigree of trees stripped of leaves at last
I observe, though no winter blast
As yet to register defeat, withering
Of the faculties, winter of the soul, ice on the heart.
Only subdued grey melancholy
Over the russet and sepia landscape,
Upon which the winter sun rises
With low and level kindness of farewell,
A rarer radiance for being touched with frost.

In Fine

THINGS have been made easy for others,
  But never for me.
Why should this be? –
That is the question.
Too uncompromising?
Too anxious to achieve?
All my life I have tried too hard,
And now that at the latter end
It might be thought
I had the ball at my feet,
I refuse to pick it up:
Instead I take
A malicious delight
In denying them,
And make
No further effort.